"Brothers, have you found our King?
There He is, kissing little children
and saying they are like God."

George McDonald

Photography by:	Page:
Ben Alex:	Front cover, 3, 9, 13, 15, 17, 21, 23, 29, 33, 35, 41, 43, 45, 49, 53, 57, 61, 63
Robert C. Hayes:	47
Roland Larsen:	64
Mauritius:	25, 51, 55
Pictor:	7
Stockphotos:	11, 19, 31, 37
Tony Stone:	5, 27, 39, 59

First published in the United States in 1986 by Thomas Nelson Publishers.
Scripture quotations are from the New King James version.
Copyright © 1979, 1980, 1982, Thomas Nelson, Inc., Publishers.

Published in Nashville, Tennessee, by Thomas Nelson, Inc. and distributed in Canada by Lawson Falle, Ltd., Cambridge, Ontario.
Printed in Singapore.
ISBN 0-8407-6699-8

MAGIC MOMENTS
In the Kingdom of Kids

Marlee & Ben Alex

publishers since 1798

THOMAS NELSON PUBLISHERS
Nashville • Camden • New York

Life Before Birth

Early morning thumps, deep down in the hollow of me, give fresh reassurance of you awaiting birth. Yesterday, my friends brought you gifts — soft, pretty things like you. Just wait! The Lord has given your Daddy and me prayers for you, too. We get wonder in our eyes, like a child, when we think of our special miracle: your conception and life.

Just ten weeks after conception you already had the physical traits of a fully developed person: ten tiny toe nails, ears like a complex labyrinth,and the most delicate nose and mouth. Your intellect and spirit cannot be measured right now, but no one can prove that they have not developed right along with fingers and toes. In fact, from the most diminutive beginning you have been full of infinite possibilities.

Tiny life, living in the darkness of a universe you don't comprehend, yet like a bud on a barren branch, you encompass all the potential of a whole world of spring.

In your silent, sheltered, aqua-world, we love you, wonderful child.

Mom

The Arrival

You entered our world as the clock in the delivery room struck 1 a.m.

I had worked late that night. Your mom called and said, "I'm going!" I hijacked a taxi and arrived from the other end of town. As I ran through the empty hospital corridors all kinds of fears and worries welled up in me as I rehearsed the four steps of labor breathing. Your mom was waiting in a bed behind a glass door. I never saw her face so torn. I whispered, "Hi, Mom."

We had prepared for you. I had managed to make a diaper shelf and a changing table in the bathroom. We had socks and pants and shirts so tiny that I refused to believe you would be able to fit them. Secretly, I had studied the babies in every baby carriage I passed. I thought I knew about baby sizes.

I had listened to the sounds from your aqua-world, felt your kicks and heard your mom tell about you. Those were the days with piles of books about pregnancy and child care on the night-table.

We had prepared your way and committed you into the hands of God. Now it was up to the doctor. I helped. Boy, how clumsy I felt. I had the camera all ready, but forgot to take the picture. Instead, your arrival is forever preserved on the retina of my heart.

You popped into my arms, and love poured through. My heart did somersaults. Ten fingers! Ten toes! And the world's softest bottom! You were blue and red and beautiful. You announced your arrival with a yelp.

As I held you in my arms, my heart was wrapping a birth gift for you: "Thank you, God. In this child I see that you are. May she become a whole person, living with integrity in her world. Create in her a spirit that will respond to your love. And may she die the day she is no longer alive."

I walked home through the night. The stars sang my heart apart. I whispered over and over, "I love you, little one." I had become something a thousand job promotions could never make me.

I had become a dad.

One of these days I am going to write all the scientists in the world and tell them I have found what they are searching for.

Dad

Baby Thoughts

Baby! You arrived on a cool and clouded evening. Welcome, oh welcome, little daughter. Daddy is held in fascination by your sweet, expressive mouth. Mommy can't stop looking into your great big, dreamy eyes, mirror of all the treasure within you. Our hearts are full beyond expression. You are beautiful, a reflection of your Creator.

After your birth I was filled with a dizzy, wondrous satisfaction that I'd never known before. I felt like the only woman on earth who had ever had a baby. For the first weeks I breast-fed you three times every night. Daddy wished he could help out. Even when he got up and changed your diaper, he mostly felt sorry for me. He never knew our secret. For the darkness and the quietness and the awesomeness of he and I having made you made the strain enchanted. I felt deep pools of peace during those moments that Daddy never knew about. He never shared those private, middle-of-the-night feelings.

By day it was more difficult. Feeding you seemed harsher. My nipples were sore. The rocking chair never seemed to fit. The telephone would ring or the dog wanted out. The piles of laundry and dishes got higher and higher. But you clucked and cooed and stroked my breast like a kitten. Sometimes you stopped sucking just long enough to smile.

Those days you were teaching me tender lessons, lessons only weakness can teach. You were interpreting for me the language of eternity.

Mom

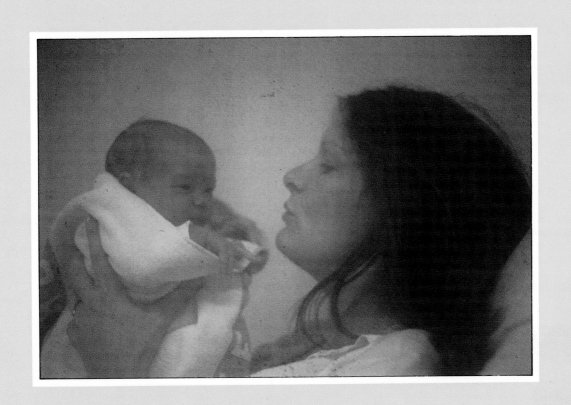

Being a Dad

1 wonder if there's something wrong with me, since I don't seem to share the same kind of intimate feelings or to draw forth the same ardent responses in you as your mother does. Sometimes I walk off confused, feeling left out. I try to be a good dad when I come home from work, but I usually end up disappointed. You don't seem to care for me the same way I care about you.

I've heard it is normal for one-and-a-half-year-old children to be attached to the one person that spends the most time with them. And I guess you're a normal one-and-a-half-year-old. But I can't wait until you get old enough to look me in the eyes and say, "Daddy, let's play!"

Believe me, it's hard to be a father these days when roles and patterns are changing. I'm trying to become a loving, learning, modern dad who can give my loved ones emotional security. Now is the time for me to learn what it really means to be a dad: to lay down my defenses and put my life into the hands of my child.

I can't force you to love me the way I love you. You may run into my arms. You may turn your back to me. Still, I will love you unconditionally and hope you someday will respond to that love.

— Dad

Magic Moments

Today I watched as you tucked your dolly into her breadpan bed. She was naked and ragged and scribbled on, but you lovingly pulled her blanket up to her chin and started to toddle away. Then you stopped suddenly with a twinkle in your eye. You looked back and whispered, "Kiss?" as you turned around to lay a smackeroo on her plastic cheek.

Moments with you are magic. Your moments of being one year old are mine, and my moments are yours. We share the timelessness of a goodnight kiss on a smudged, dimpled left cheek. You inspire me to want to be a better woman. You convince me of the unsurpassed importance of relationships, and of cultivating rich ones.

Because of you, I want to learn more about friendship and about prayer. I want to invest more in learning Scripture and in learning a new idea or a new skill every day. I want to develop my sense of humor. I want to improve my creative abilities. I want to be less passive in making my dreams come true, and more active in helping you and your daddy to realize yours.

I hope you won't grow up thinking of me in terms of what I do, but in terms of who I am, in terms of my thoughts, feelings, and responses to the world around me. I want us to take the ordinary moments and make them magic.

I hope you will keep that twinkle in your eye as you grow up. I hope you will keep looking back occasionally to draw inspiration from your roots. For someday I'm sure someone else will discover the timelessness of a goodnight kiss on your dimpled left cheek and I'll have to let you go.

The magic moments will belong to him.

Mom

With God We are All Beginners

T his morning you saw God outside your bedroom window.

"He was white all over, Daddy," you said with a certainty and a simplicity that made me sneak out to check.

To you God is not that complicated. You're so certain about his love and so simple in accepting his mysteries.

There is a joy that comes to those who allow God to be mysterious and real at the same time. Together with you, I explore that kind of joy. Together we talk to God about everything, and we wonder about the questions that seem to have no answer.

As you grow up you'll start to reason. You'll find you need answers that can satisfy your mind. But don't lose the joy of mystery and never feel ashamed to say, "I cannot explain; I just know." In the midst of the unexplainable you'll get to know him better, he who created the unexplainable, and love him. That's the mystery of our faith.

To learn to reason will prepare you for death. To learn to love will prepare you for life. Through you I've learned an important lesson: with God we're both beginners.

Dad

14

Days of Soap and Plum Blossoms

1 wonder what your earliest memory is. I have so many. I think my favorite one is when you were two. We had a big vegetable garden that summer. Daddy planted rows and rows of peas behind the raspberry bushes. I planted a big corn patch that grew up way over your head and mine.

I know it rained a lot that summer. I know I pulled a lot of weeds. But what I remember most vividly is you with sunlight in your curls and mud on your blue overalls, standing in the middle of the pea vines. You had fistfulls of pods, stuffing the tiny, green balls into your mouth.

Our neighbor made you a go-cart that summer. The grass in our yard grew thick. There was a little black lamb born to our flock. I hung up diapers every other day while you swung under the porch. The days smelled of soap and plum blossoms.

Together, you and I are memory gardeners. The seeds sown in your childhood will one day nurture your spirit and soul as an adult. We may raise some weeds along with the fruit, but with patience and care, our yesterdays will become cherished dreams of happiness.

We will harvest memories through the years, and find that the sweetest ones grow in our own backyard.

Mom

Saying "Yes"

Sometimes I am disillusioned about parenthood. It wasn't exactly what I expected it to be. I thought we could have a peaceful little family, go on idyllic Sunday picnics, and always be positive and loving toward each other.

It didn't work out that way. Soon I found myself shouting and yelling at you. "Close that door!" "Stop that noise!" "How many times have I told you...!" I hated it. It only took fifteen minutes for me to run out of patience with you. And when I came home in the evening after a busy day we were both tired and irritable.

I remember the night you were born. It was a miracle that made me realize God still has grace left for this earth. And as you grew I realized how much grace was needed in your particular case. I often asked God to help me become a better steward of his grace to you. I felt lousy, because it seemed like I spent more time yelling at you than in building up a loving relationship with you.

One Saturday morning you stood at my bed (very early) and said, "Dad, let's build a ship!" That particular morning, like most mornings, I had other important things to do. But somehow we ended up in the garage with tools all over the floor—building a ship.

That morning I promised myself that I'll say "yes" more than I'll say "no". You're a person that requires terribly many "no's", but my promise helped me be more creative about the "yes's".

I believe that the more I say "yes" to you (when there's not a good reason to say "no"), the more you'll respond to me, and to God and the world around you in the same way later on.

You won't have any false paternal images to rebel against.

Dad

Hyperactive?

You used to scream in stubborn fury whenever I tried to feed you at the hospital where you were born. "She's got quite a temperament," the nurses told me. I had to milk-out and forcefeed you with a bottle. Then as soon as we came home, you wanted nothing else but to breast-feed every two hours.

They told me that small babies slept most of the time. You didn't know that. And you didn't take to just lying in your cradle, either. Mobiles, toys, and bright shiny bobbles didn't help. At just a few weeks old, you fussed and squirmed and whined if you were not within eyesight of me and if I didn't talk or sing or touch you. I dubbed night-times as your own special form of torture.

The terrible-two's developed early, and I, who had been wondering if you were hyperactive, became convinced of it. All those other moms with toddlers seemed proud. "My baby began to crawl at six months, walk at nine months, and now she's into everything!" I could identify with the last part until it dawned on me there was a vast chasm between what those other moms considered "everything", and what "everything" really meant. Not long afterwards you started forming sentences out of words. From that point on, your constant movement was matched by incessant chatter and questions.

I read scores of books and magazine articles, gleaning ideas to help me cope. The advice sounded good in print, but proved mostly useless. I took consolation in the one expert who said, "Your child is unique. Accept her as she is." And so, I stopped expecting you to fit into the patterns someone else had defined as normal, and started seeing the positive side of all that energy.

I have heard it said that there are three kinds of people in this world: those who make things happen, those who watch what happens, and those who don't know what's happening. You definitely classify in the first category. And someday when you are out there changing the world, I suppose I'll look back on these frantic days of mothering you as the best investment I ever made.

Mom

Growing Conscience

So often I feel drained and exhausted after putting you to bed at night. We probably have the two most difficult hours of the day together: between the time I come home at five and the time you go to bed at seven.

I feel tempted to use power to make you do what I say. I know you were born with a strong will, and I know your kind of personality finds its security in bouncing against the boundaries to test them.

Still, I'd rather go back to my chair feeling the exhaustion of the struggle than the shallow satisfaction of having forced you to obey. There are people who turn their children into robots by using power, threats, or bribes. It must be terrible to be responsible for having created a perfect creature with nice manners by crushing his spirit and robbing him of initiative, creativity, and joy.

Last night I had to do something unusual. I had to spank you because I couldn't get through to you in any other way. Afterwards you said, "I like my tears, Daddy. They taste good."

I hope that in the long run, I can bend that strong will of yours and still allow you to feel completely yourself around me. I want you to be you, but I also want you to know right from wrong.

Along the way I hope we can grow the fragile, little flower inside you called conscience.

Dad

Let's have a Party

"Mommy, I think we should tell all my friends it's my birthday and send them a birthday card and a present."

You were almost three. I started to explain to you that birthdays are for receiving gifts. My better judgment prevailed, however. If I could have bottled the way you felt that day, I would have. And I would sprinkle it on your head like stardust every birthday for the rest of your life.

You will have to grow up like the rest of us. You will have to discover that you, too, need the grace of God. You will have to make moral choices that for my generation would have been unthinkable. Your need for a stabilizing force in your life will be greater than mine. It will be necessary that your roots grow deeper, just as the possibilities of your life extend further.

I feel awed and humbled by my role in your life. I'm not the greatest mom, but I'm the best you've got. And I rest on the knowledge that God must have believed I could handle the challenge of raising you. Other televison and magazine moms tell me that staying home and raising my own children is a luxury society cannot afford. They say it's more important to think about myself first, and that you, little one, will be better off for it anyway.

Sometimes I listen to them. Sometimes I believe them. Sometimes I long for a great big party celebrating me for a change (and lots of presents tied with fancy bows!). Sometimes...until your face lights up in anticipation of all that you can give away. Your innocence is the most eloquent reminder of the real reason God gave us birthdays.

Thank you. You are the most precious gift of all.

Mom

Responding to Your Feelings

You're a talker. Whatever enters your mind exits through your mouth, so I often tend to ignore what you're saying.

Today I set aside a special time with you. We went out to a restaurant together, alone. I tried to respond to every word you said because this was a time especially for you. I tried to understand your childish emotions. We had a great time, and we felt closer on the way home.

I cannot always be present like that. But I realized today how important it really is for you and me to spend time alone together. I realized that listening to your feelings is more important than hearing what you say.

I often bring you a gift when I return from a trip. But it's more important that I respond to you than that I stimulate you. The best gifts I can give you are time and presence. It's fun to be together. We don't want to let all the good things happen outside the boundaries of our own family.

I would like to do things with you that we can both enjoy more often, instead of just doing things out of obligation. And I realize how important it is for you that we spend part of that time in your own room.

Before you went to sleep tonight, we lay in your bed and counted spots on the ceiling.

Dad

26

Never Lost in Secondness

The look in your eyes when we pass the candy counter at the grocer's is just like that in mine when I peer into the jewelry store window. In spite of knowing that those wonderful things are absolutely out of reach, your gaze is filled with wonder. You dream of candy like I dream of diamonds and pearls.

But diamonds and pearls are shoddy merchandise compared to the treasures that I'm gathering. They are not the store-bought kind. They are the genuine ones that will last forever. Your life is a gift to the world, and I am the one who gets to unwrap the package.

I will always carry with me the peace, quietness and confidence of those moments before you made your appearance. The lights in the delivery room were dimmed. The midwife gave me a warm hug. And afterwards, I watched Daddy holding you in his arms. He whispered over and over, "We love you, Baby."

The wonder of your existence will never be lost in secondness. I find that my heart is still expectant. And in your gentle coming you conceived within it a new universe of treasures, fragile treasures that could easily be aborted if I did not remain aware of what makes you, *you.*

Among the treasures that I gather is the poignant memory of the night you were born, the sticky giggles and pink rosebud smiles of toddler times, the crazy ecstasy in your eyes when Daddy comes home and rubs your cheek with his frosty beard, the expressions of tender pain when you watch an oh-so-sad episode of "Little House on the Prairie," and those contented sighs when I dance you to sleep or kiss your toes.

The treasures that I gather are not material illusions. Among my favorites is that look of wonder in your eyes when we pass the candy counter at the grocer's.

—Mom

Jesus in your Heart

You were not quite five. You bounced up on my bed beside the patchwork pieces I was laying out and asked, "Mommy, can I ask Jesus into my heart?" Your tousled hair and smudged face were a picture of comic relief. But as we talked about what asking Jesus into your heart was all about, I realized that your childish spirit was sincere and ready. And so we prayed. I felt thankful and awe-struck that God could make himself understood by a child.

"How can you know that Jesus lives in your heart now?" I asked, assuming your answer would somehow be wiser than your years.

"Ouch, I can feel his leg!" you chirped.

I guess God smiled just like I did. Why should I expect a fully sprung blossom of knowledge and faith in you? What do I know of the personal things God is doing or is going to do in his own special relationship with you? I do know his seed is now planted in your heart.

I am going to nourish that seed with my prayers, and to water it with God's Word, one drop at a time. I want to resist the temptation to expect you to be just like me, as well as the temptation to give you easy answers before you have struggled with the questions.

I hope I can be an inspiration to you. But I hope you will take more risks, climb higher, and know God better than I ever have. One day, the tender shoot from this seed we sowed beside my patchwork pieces will break through the surface and have to meet the challenges to its survival. I will always believe in your ability to meet those challenges honestly and at your own pace.

Meanwhile, I delight in the Jesus in you, unique and unrepeatable!

Mom

30

Failures and Successes

 am sorry. I made a mistake when you came home with your grades. I noticed the bad grades first. Why am I so concerned about your failures that I tend to overlook your successes?

Let's pretend we have two baskets. The one on this side is for the "goods". The one on the other side is for the "bads". Let's find out what you're good at and put it in the basket with "goods".

You're good at painting, spelling, and at expressing yourself verbally. You feel responsible, especially for your little sister, and you're good at inventing new games to play. And I think if we try to find more things, we'll find lots that you're good at.

You're still not so good at math, or listening to others, or ballet lessons. And I think there are a few other things which you will improve.

Let me tell you about the time I was learning to play the trumpet. I was twelve years old. There was a concert and I was to blow the fanfare right when the orchestra paused to breathe. It was supposed to sound like this: "Tra-tra-ta-ta-ta-ta". I had practiced for weeks. But as the moment for my solo approached, my mouth started to dry up and my lips began to tremble. I lifted the trumpet, and the orchestra paused.

Not a sound came out of that thing and everybody knew that I blew it because the program read: "Solo by Ben Alex". I felt terrible afterwards. Weeks passed before I picked up the trumpet again.

Eventually I realized that it is okay to fail, and that if we concentrate on what we're good at rather than dwelling on our failures, yesterday's failures will become less important. We will visualize our tomorrows in the light of our successes.

The basket with "goods" is heavier than the one with "bads".

The Closeness of Heaven

One of our neighbors, a young mother of two, is suffering a terminal illness and is lying close to death. I wonder, if it were me who were dying, what would I feel? And how would I communicate my feelings to you? There are nights when I wake up and can't get back to sleep because of the longing to hold you close to me and protect you from hurt and fear.

Some people ask, "Why bring children into a dying world like ours at all?" I once read the story of a first-century Christian woman who was condemned by the Romans to be thrown to the wild beasts. She was pregnant, and so, won permission to wait in prison until the birth of her child. She used this time to write, not about remorse, darkness and death, but about beauty, light and life. In her cruel world she gave birth to more than a child. She gave birth to hope and to faith and to a kingdom that was to be borne in the hearts of men.

Your life, little one, is destined not only to meet good and evil here on earth, but is a promise of more to follow: eternity with God and his son, Jesus. Can you understand at all how close Heaven is? If we could see the beauty that begins when our natural bodies die, surely we would run and leap into it with open arms.

Even so, eternal life has already begun for us. We do not have to wait for death to make us aware of its reality. And as long as you and I remain in the love of God and his Son, nothing, not even death, can separate us.

— Mom

34

Learning to Fly

It was Sunday morning. We stood barefoot at the back door. A summer breeze rippled the grain fields beyond our garden. The sky was blue, like an old enamel coffee pot. We spotted a lark against the window of the universe.

You said, "Daddy, I wish I was a bird. Then I could fly away when a lion comes."

That day we built a kite and watched it learn to fly. You held the string tight. It looked like an unending umbilical cord up through the sky.

The kite made dips and dives as it climbed higher and higher. It was fighting for its freedom. The string cut into your small hands. You tried so hard to hold it steady, but it stung your fingers and kept on tugging away. At last you realized you could not pull it back.

You had to let go.

As we walked home over the hills you said, "I wish I hadn't cut it loose. I wish I still had my kite." I squeezed your hand.

If you really love something and want to hold onto it, you have to let go. You have to run the risk of losing it, or it will never really be yours.

You may not understand that now, but one day in years to come, you may walk hand in hand with a child. And then you will.

Dad

Some of
God's Miracles Are Small

Now that the trees are bare, I can just see you in your sandbox behind the hedge of plum trees from the kitchen window. I'm thankful for the warm haven of our kitchen where I can watch you playing undisturbed. You seem to thrive in all the cold, wet sandy mess surrounded by multitudes of pots and pans, spoons and shovels.

I can't help smiling to myself as I watch you. You tirelessly repeat the same movements again and again. You mix the sand, pour it into another cup, scoop it out, mix it up, dump it out, spoon it in again. How you remind me of myself! Going about my round of monotonous household duties day after day, I use most of my limited energy doing the same tasks over and over. I have wearied of it sometimes, but you help me see it in a bright new perspective.

Even if I could rank as a super-homemaker and mom, or successfully manage a professional career with motherhood, I would still be lonely at the resurrection unless I allowed my life to be transformed in the small things. The things that I do in love are the only things I'll take with me into eternity.

I recently read a quip by a popular feminist. She said, "Any woman can have a child, but only I can write my books."

I reply, "Any woman can write books, but only I can have my child." The small things are full of greatness and dignity. The unseen, unborn things are sacred. These are the eternal things upon which we should spend our love. It is from the small things in my life I learn the most.

I can just see one of them from my kitchen window.

— Mom

A New Day

1 n a moment you'll wake with a start, ready to explore a new day. The excitement you feel. The colors you see. The enchantment. The vague memories of yesterday. The doll whose name was Gigi when you tucked her in last night. Who knows what her name will be today? Who knows what new games you'll play?

Your world is one of magic, merry-go-rounds and cotton candy. It's hard for me to get into your world, but sometimes I find a little door and crawl through on my knees, just as Alice did to get into Wonderland.
Behind the door I feel so small, but something in me grows; a little boy who napped for years comes alive at the age of five. Together we're lost in Wonderland.

I want the enchantment to stay with you as long as possible. In today's electronic world you are so easily and prematurely rushed into adulthood. The outside world is pushed upon you in pictures you read. But I want to protect you from a reality that is too big to go through your door.

There's no need for answers when you don't yet know what the questions are.

Hidden Treasure Of the Heart

Tonight you dutifully ate your quartered tomatoes. I speared each of them on the fork and put them in your mouth. As you started to gag with each bite, I told you they were full of sunshine and they were yummy and wonderful on such a snowy day. After that you didn't gag. You just said, "Say 'sunshine'," every time you opened your mouth. Your dark eyes sparkled underneath those straight shaggy bangs. I could have kept on feeding you quartered tomatoes all night.

Last Sunday morning the bickering began as usual over who was to get the first, the biggest, and the most pieces of bacon. I reminded you and your sister that when we get to heaven, God is not going to ask who got the biggest piece of bacon, but who was the first to give it away. A silence fell over the table. A look of contrition crossed your face. Then you quietly reached up and placed your small piece of bacon over on your sister's plate.

You charm me. No matter how disenchanting your circumstances, I know that you will always be able to transform them by your sense of wonder. No matter how little you have, I know that you will always have enough to give away.

Unlike so many of the rest of us who are still searching for the map, you have already uncovered the hidden treasure.

Mom

Stories And Scary Dreams

D addy, tell me a story!"

That's your favorite refrain. You love stories. For a while you wanted to hear stories about when I was a little boy, but your first interruption would come after the opening sentence, "How old were you, Dad?"

There were other times when you preferred books of fantasy and fairy tales. You would listen to them again and again.

When I think back, my fondest memories of childhood are the times I sat on my grandmother's lap and listened to her stories. My favorite story was the one about Little Red Riding Hood. When we came to the point where Riding Hood says, "What a big mouth you have," I would close my eyes and not open them again until the hunter came and rescued her.

I loved my grandmother, and I cried the day they laid her in the earth. But her stories stayed with me during all these years. Now I realize that her stories were more than just entertainment. They were tools in my attempt to make order out of my world, and in my coming to terms with reality.

On special occasions my grandmother would read from a black book filled with pictures. I loved to look at the pictures, but I felt excited and afraid at the same time because there were pictures I didn't want to see, yet couldn't help peeking at: Cain killing his brother Abel, Abraham holding a knife over his son Isaac, John the Baptist's head on a silver platter.

Grandmother taught me that stories don't necessarily have happy endings. Violence is a part of life, and so are growing pains, scary dreams and dark rooms. Through her stories, Grandmother taught me that life is a course between God's warnings and God's promises.

Now it's my turn to pass the stories on and to offer quiet moments of warmth, wonder and wisdom. Tonight you insisted on having the light on, " 'cause the darkness comes into my eyes so I can't see."

Dad

Little Mommy, Growing Mommy

Mommies have growing pains too. We do not come factory assembled. Mommies sometimes have to stretch and hurt and endure because, as yet, no cherry-flavored aspirin has been invented for grown-ups suddenly plummeted into parenthood. Mommies may seem big to you, but it doesn't come easily.

When you were four I shed a lot of growing-up tears. It seemed impossible to manage a stubborn, opinionated little girl. Just when I was getting a handle on it, you began to blossom into a harmonious five year old. You started to call me affectionately "Little Mommy", and seemed to understand that mommies need hugs too (at least four a day to survive, and twelve a day to grow on!).

Now, on this unrelentlessly drizzly day, you inquire of your frazzled little mommy, "Do you remember the time we filled all those water balloons to throw at Daddy and then we got wetter than he did?" Oh yes, I remember. And I think I recognize your tactful reminder that to be silly again is just what we both need, right here and now.

I always believed that growing up meant becoming more responsible. But if that is the only direction I grow, I'll end up with a crooked spine. On the other hand, one of the most responsible things I've ever done may very well be that time I laid down my paring knife and walked away from the kitchen just at supper-time. I filled 35 water balloons and joined you on the front porch to wait for Daddy's appearance through the gate. That day, with a splattering, rubbery wet smash against my sweaty skin, I rediscovered a special kind of growing-pain reliever. Or was it a growth tonic?

So on this unrelentlessly drizzly day when Mommy's in a frazzle, if you are beginning to doubt that being a grown-up is something you ever want to be, just wait until I put away my mop. Grab your umbrella and rubber boots. The puddles look inviting. And we just might discover a brand new definition of growing up!

Mom

Becoming Friends

Last night Mom and I had a fight because we disagreed over something. You heard it, and I want to explain to you what was going on.

But first I want you to know that the fight had nothing to do with you.

Sometimes Mom and I disagree, and may even get angry, since we're ordinary people that want to grow closer together. You cannot grow closer without disagreeing, and it's not wrong to argue. Some people even need an argument to find out what they are disagreeing about.

An argument has a beginning, a middle and an ending. Just like fairy tales. The most important part is the ending.

You do not have to avoid conflicts with other people. Conflicts help you grow. But you always need to respect the other person's opinions and feelings, and to work towards a happy ending.

That's how friendships are built.

Back to Normal

You are almost six. I can get back to normal now. But what is normal? I'm not sure I know anymore. For more than five years my time has been consumed by little needs. Mine was the ministry of interruptions, a constant flow of them day and night.

Gradually, spare moments have evolved. Sometimes I have the time to stop and think, to make a choice about what to do next, to do things I never had time for before, like cleaning the graham cracker crumbs out of my coat pockets or looking for the pieces of Daddy's scattered chess set. I even have golden moments when it crosses my mind that maybe it's possible to get-it-all-together after all.

I've heard that as children grow older, the demands they make on you change, but are just as time consuming; and that teenagers need less instruction or being talked at, but more time spent by someone who will listen to them. When I opted to be a mom, I'll admit that I didn't know what it would take out of me. I expected to retain at least a thread of normality throughout the process. But now I know the truth. Normality doesn't exist. Five years does a lot of changing. There is no going back.

Thank goodness for that. The tedious trivialities of motherhood have made me aware of a new reality. The interruptions of life are pregnant with unexpected opportunities. When you call, "Mommy" (just once more!) and run through the house — brand new shoes all muddied up — I look for something deeper, and I discover the stars dancing in your eyes. For you found a sea shell in our (freshly sown) garden!

Mom

Ballet Lessons And Other Necessities of Life

I know you don't love it and that you'd probably prefer to jump into mud puddles in the street. But we've decided you're going to learn things we didn't have the chance to learn. You'd better be happy that it's only one ballet lesson a week, because later on you'll take piano lessons too.

Since you are only five, you pretty well accept ballet lessons as a fact of life, but later when you start piano, you'll have reached an age when you think we're old-fashioned and unreasonable, maybe.

I took piano lessons when I was ten. Later on I also took trumpet lessons. A stern trumpet teacher made me stand on a newspaper in front of the note holder in his living room so that I would not get spit on his carpet.

Now I'm glad that my parents insisted on the lessons. And here's the reason I'm insisting on yours too. There will be days later on in life when you'll feel lonely or depressed. There may be a lot of people around you and there may be many words spoken to you. But they will not bring you comfort. That will be the time to communicate along with the masters, to speak the language of art in order to receive what cannot be bought, begged or borrowed.

You may never become a ballerina or a concert pianist. That's fine. But I want you to learn the basics in disciplining the way you express yourself, and I want you to learn a variety of expressions. Along the way you may receive new visions for your own life and enough inspiration to pass on to somebody else.

Dad

My Special Unexpected Child

Before I ever dreamt about your coming to be part of our family, I had lined up plans and projects and was eager to get started on them. I had set goals for myself which required a concentrated effort. I had taken on responsibilities that demanded my maximum time. My plans were shattered and all my projects came to a halt when I realized that you were on the way.

It seems absurd now to remember the devastation I felt then. You seemed to come into my heart backwards. One hour before you were born, I was once more devastated to learn that you were in breech position. You were to come backwards into my world as well. Labor was turbulent, just as my heart had been in the beginning of pregnancy.

At long last, your head was born, and I saw your small, pink face. In that moment of relief and joy, fear and disappointment were dispelled in a way I cannot explain. It is like a secret between God and myself. How thankful I am that he didn't allow me to live out my life without you.

Conception is a miracle, but your conception is a special one because it led to a transformation of my spirit as well as my life. What I believed was an inconvenient, ill-timed step backward was in reality an avenue to renewal. You are not only an unexpected bonus, you are a gift from a very wise God who is involved in the minutest details of our lives.

My previous plans may have been sidetracked, but now I have new ones. My energy may be depleted, but my cup of joy is filled to the brim. I could have completed my projects and reached my goals. Your Dad and I could have, by now, been out of debt, conquered our exhaustion, written that dream-novel, spent a precious bit more time and money on your big sisters. However, not a one of us could have been happier or richer than we are right now, with your smile lighting up our home.

On judgment day when all the dross has been burned away from my life, there will, hopefully, be a bit of my life's work remaining. But you are pure gold. You are a treasure I will carry with me into Heaven, along with the magnificent awareness that God's greatest miracle can happen in my own heart.

Mom

A Promise of God

Joy is your name.

We chose that name against the odds. I'm glad we did. Through you we are reminded that weeping is always followed by joy, that resurrection always follows death. We received you as a promise of God.

"A woman, when she is in labor, has sorrow because her hour has come; but as soon as she has given birth to the child, she no longer remembers the anguish, for joy that a human being has been born into the world" (John 16:21).

To some people the value of children is measured against education, career and material things. Our neighbors decided not to have a baby. They went to the South Pacific instead. We went to garage sales for a crib and a high chair.

You know, I wouldn't trade a promise of God for anything in this world. In the night you wake up and laugh to yourself. In the dark you giggle and babble. "Da-da." Then silence. You lie and wonder where the sound came from. Then you try again. "Da-da-da." You go on like that for hours until one of us gives in to sleep.

To be a father is to embrace a promise, to see the important in what's invisible to the eye, to love without having to find a reason. This is the greatest spiritual experience a man can have. Only through a child can a man understand the heart of God. This was what Abraham, the Father of Faith, experienced. God taught him who He was by making him a father.

You don't know it, but in the dark nights I listen, and my heart bursts with joy.

That's the way God must feel when, in the darkness, we cry out: "Da-da."

Time Enough for Everything

I have just joined the ranks of "working" mothers. (As if I was not working before!) Our bulging budget couldn't stretch any further,so I have been forced into earning a paycheck. Much to my surprise and in spite of the initial adjustment, I've discovered that I love my paid work as much as I love homemaking, and besides this, it has brought to a halt my complaints that there are not enough hours in my day.

I've chosen a job I can do at home, juggling my duties to fit your schedules. The pace is hard, but the challenge of winning the battle against time is heady. It forces me to be better organized and to expect more of you. Sometimes I feel like the skipper at the helm of a heaving ship in choppy waters. I navigate the rising tides of laundry and dust, and reel in the hurricanes created by your growing natural energies while clinging to my chain of thought so that I can ease in "work" between baby pit-stops and unexpected waves of telephone calls, sudden illness, auto failure, quarrels, bumps and broken hearts.

Little by little it has become obvious that not only is it possible to survive all this, but it is in facing these challenges with faith that I liberate reserves of strength to match my multiplied responsibilities. Drawing upon the power of God, the pressure can be transformed into an asset; for the outward hassles are no hindrance to my enthusiasm for you. They force me to maintain it more fervently than ever. The real hindrances come from within: resentment, boredom, resignation.

The increased pressure gives me leverage to take charge, to create a constructive course for the day before the day takes charge of me. It compels me to act upon the belief that a positive, affirming attitude in our home is more important than its furnishings, that the people in our home are more important than the jobs we do. The urgent practicalities that have to be done will somehow always get done. I am learning to save my emotional energy so that I can squander it on the important things.

There really is time enough for everything, even time enough for the meticulous mending of broken hearts. But it took a shorter day to convince me that it's true!

Mom

Trying the Impossible

1 love it when you want to try something new. There are always reasons to repeat what you already know, to choose the same path as you chose yesterday. But those reasons do not outnumber the reasons to do things differently today.

Sometimes you may feel like quitting, and that's okay; like the time we went to the park to try out your new bicycle and you couldn't ride it right away. But I'm not suggesting that you should sit on the sidelines and watch as life and people pass by. It's not up to you to make the choice. Life chooses you.

You'd better hang in there by making the best out of it. Let your willingness to explore and take risks overcome comfort, security and boredom while pursuing the impossible.

The experts are finally discovering that creativity quotient is more important than intelligence quotient. But somebody told me that when a person is 40 years old there is only two percent of the creativity left which he had as a child. It doesn't have to be that way. Playfulness is the key.

"My dad does a lot of silly things!" I heard you say that to Emily.

I think that's the nicest compliment I've ever had.

For of Such Is the Kingdom

As your mom, my ambition is to sculpt places in your heart for the important things and to communicate the kingdom of God to you. But at the rate you're growing and the speed I'm going I often wonder how effective my efforts are going to be.

Moses encouraged the Hebrews to teach their children about the Lord from the first waking moments of every day. At home and away from home, they were to take advantage of vulnerable moments, interweaving the commandments with daily routine. It seems that passing along a holy heritage has always required something beyond formal teaching. Laughter and play have always been the best inroads to the souls and spirits of children.

Sometimes I take myself too seriously as a parent. Sometimes I become a detriment to my own best ambitions. But I'm learning. I pick myself up, dust off the residue of my mistakes, try again and learn over and over again. The most amazing thing I'm learning is that when I laugh and play with you, it is my own soul and spirit that gain the most. It is me who needs the laughter and the play, the tickling and the giggling before bedtime. It is me who needs *you*.

Like the time I got lost among Austrian foothills and then stumbled upon a meadow af sunny wildflowers, I never expected to discover anything quite so wonderful when I stumbled clumsily into the kingdom of kids. When I reach out and hug you, sticky faces 'n all, I embrace the kingdom of God and encounter its creative power within me.

For the kingdom of God is you!

Mom

Let the little
children come to me,
and do not forbid them;
for of such
is the kingdom
of heaven.

(Matt. 19:14)